hair Wraps

By Anne Akers Johnson

KLUTZ.

Getting
Started

Spirals

pg 26

The
Basic
Wrap

pg 6

Stripes

pg 11

X's

pg 20

Adding
Charms

pg 10

Adding
Beads

pg 12

Rope
Wrap

pg 18

Woven
Wrap

pg 22

Chaining
Beads

pg 14

hair wraps

3

Getting Started

Wrapping your
own hair is a little
tricky, so find a friend
who will trade wraps
with you. Most wraps
last anywhere from a
couple of days to
a couple of weeks,
depending on how
tightly you wrap,
how often you wash
your hair, and the
texture of your hair.
It is fine to wash your
hair normally while
wearing a wrap.

1 Choose a skinny section of hair, about like this:

2 Divide the section of hair into three strands, and cross the left strand over the center...

3 ...then cross the right strand over the center.

It will be easiest to work on your hair wrap if you first braid the section of hair you're wrapping. Try getting the strand wet before braiding it, or coating it with a little gel. This will keep stray hairs from poking out.

4 Repeat these two steps until the strand is completely braided. Tie a short piece of floss at the end of the braid to hold it. Don't worry about the color of this thread, you'll take it out later.

TIP Pull all of your hair back, leaving just the section you want to wrap hanging free. If you're wrapping a section of hair on the top of the head, pin a tissue to the hair under the braid. This will keep stray hair from getting tangled in your wrap.

the
basic wrap

You can use as many colors of thread in your wrap as you want, though it's best to start with no more than three. You can always add more colors later. Once you get the hang of it all, change colors as often as you'd like.

1. Start with three threads, each about 48 inches long.

2. Tie the first thread onto the very top of the braid. The two ends should be the same length.

3. Tie the other threads on in the same way, just below the first.

4. Pick up one strand of the top thread...

5. ...and wrap it tightly around the hair — and the other threads — a few times.

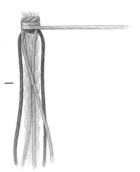

6. After four or five wraps, pick up the other thread of this color. From here on out, you will always wrap with two threads at once.

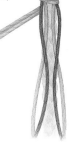

Changing colors

1.

To change the color of your wrap, hold the first color down against the braid and pick up the two threads of the color you want to use next.

2.

Begin wrapping with these threads, being sure to cover all the loose threads.

Adding thread part-way through

HINT: If you think you have just enough thread to finish your wrap, add more. It's always better to end with too much thread than not enough.

1. If you run out of a color of thread, or if you decide to add a color, simply tie the new thread on just as you did in the beginning.

2. Wrap one of the existing colors around it to cover the knot, and you're ready to use it anytime.

Holding knots

To tie a holding knot, tuck the ends of the wrapping thread under the last wrap and pull them all the way through.

To make your wrap last longer, tie holding knots every once in a while. The more you tie, the longer your wrap will last, and the harder it will be to take out. You can also tie a holding knot if you want to take a break.

Ending your wrap

1. Wrap until the hair is completely covered, then tie two holding knots. (Remove the little tie at the end of the braid if it's still there.)

2. Twist all the loose threads together and tie them in one knot close to the end of your wrap.

3. Trim the ends to about a half an inch.

Removing your wrap: Unless you've tied a lot of holding knots, your wrap will loosen and fall out in a few days. If you want to take it out earlier, carefully snip the finishing knot, then unwind the thread. Ask someone else to do this for you, and be sure to point the scissors away from your face.

Adding Charms

You can add charms to any wrap. Add them just to the end, or along the whole wrap if you want.

1 Simply poke your wrapping threads through the loop on the charm....

2 ...and continue wrapping.

3 It's best to wrap about a half an inch before you add another charm.

STRIPES

You can make stripes by wrapping with two differently colored threads at the same time.

ADDING BEADS

You can add beads to the end of any wrap. Add one, or several.

1
Wrap until all of the hair is covered, then tie two tight holding knots (see page 9).

2
Trim all the threads even, 3-4 inches below the holding knot. Twist all the threads together...

3
...then thread the bead onto the wrap.

4
Tie the threads in one tight knot close to the end of the wrap.

5
Trim the ends to within a half an inch of knot.

HINT

If you're having a hard time getting the threads through your bead: Loop a short piece of scrap thread around all your threads and poke it through the bead. Tug on the loop and it will pull all the threads through.

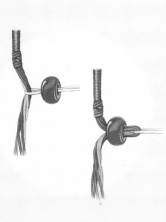

Spiral wrap shown on page 26.

Chaining Beads

*This is a more complicated way
to attach beads, but it's well worth the effort.
If you use this finish, your wrap will be longer than your
hair. Plan on having at least six pretty long pieces of thread
left at the end of your* 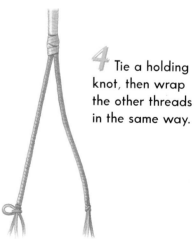 *wrap to make a chain.*

1 Wrap until all of the
hair is covered, then tie
two tight holding knots.

2 Decide what color you
want your chain to be, then
divide your threads in half,
making sure that there is
at least one long thread
of this color in each half.

3 Pick up one of these
threads, and wrap it
tightly around the other
threads in this half.
Make this skinny wrap
about 1½ inches long
if you plan to add one
bead, 2½ inches long
to add two.

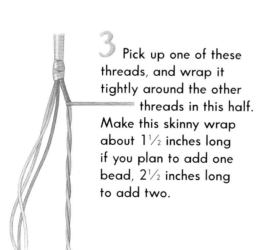

4 Tie a holding
knot, then wrap
the other threads
in the same way.

5 Poke one of the wrapped sections through the bead. It is easiest if you fold the wrapped section and push it through as shown.

Pull this wrap all the way through the bead.

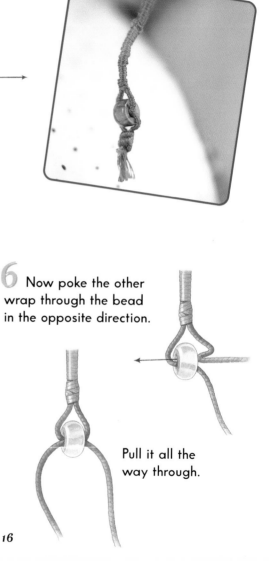

Hint: Use an extra piece of thread as shown on page 13 if you're having a hard time threading the bead.

6 Now poke the other wrap through the bead in the opposite direction.

Pull it all the way through.

*Repeat steps 5-6
if you want to add
another bead.*

7 To end
your wrap,
gather the
two wraps
together and
tie in one
tight knot.

8 Trim the
ends of your
thread to
within a half
an inch of the
finishing knot.

17

Rope wrap

1

You'll need at least three threads for this wrap.

Make a basic wrap at least a half an inch long.

2

Lift the four under-threads out of the way, and wrap at least 3 inches. Tie a holding knot at the end of this section.

3

Now go back to the four threads you left behind. Twist them together...

4

...and coil them around your wrap.

5

Pick up your wrapping threads and wrap them over the rope to hold it in place.

Wrap at least a half an inch before starting a new rope or ending your wrap.

X's

For this wrap, begin by tying on at least three threads.

1

Start
your basic
wrap as
always,
wrapping
a half
an inch
before
you start
making X's.

2

When
you're
ready to
start
your
design, lift
up four
threads
and continue
to wrap,
leaving these
threads free.

3

After
wrapping
about
2-3
inches,
tie a
holding
knot.

4

Pull your
four loose
threads
to the
front of
the wrap
and divide
in two.

5

Now wrap the
two sections
of thread
back around
the wrap,
in opposite
directions.
Look at the
picture to be
sure you've
got this right.

6

Continue
wrapping
like this,
crossing the
threads in
both the
front and
the back to
make X's.

7

When you've
reached the
end of the
wrapped
section,
simply bring
the threads
together in
the center,
and wrap
over them
to hold them
in place.

woven *Wrap*

This wrap takes a little more time than most of the others.
Tie on four threads to start. We've only used three colors, repeating one,
for this pattern. It'll be easiest if you do the
same thing your first time through.

Start a basic
wrap as always,
wrapping at
least a half an
inch before you
start weaving.

Arrange the loose
threads as you want
them to show up
on the wrap, then
wrap over them a
few times to hold
them in place.

To begin
the weave,
lift the center
color up...

...and make
two complete
wraps under it.

Lay these threads down against the hair, and lift the two outside colors up.

Make two complete wraps under these threads.

Lay the outside colors down and lift the center color again...

... and make two complete wraps under it.

Repeat steps 4-6 until the woven section is as long as you want it. End with about a half an inch of the basic wrap before knotting it off.

Once you've got this wrap down, experiment with different weaves. You can weave just one or two threads and can change the length of the weave by wrapping a few more times before changing colors.

Spirals

This wrap is more time consuming than the others, but the result is beautiful.

You'll find it hard to take out, even if you've only worn it for a short time. For this reason,

don't do this wrap unless you're willing to eventually cut the wrap off, hair and all.

1 Start with one thread, about 24 inches long. Tie one end of the thread at the very top of the section of hair being wrapped. Note that this time you have one short end of thread and one very long end of thread.

2 Loop the long thread around the hair as shown to tie a knot.

Short end

3 Pull this knot tight.

 Continue making knots exactly like this, always knotting on the same side of the wrap, even as it starts to twist. Knot over the loose end of the thread.

 Add colors in the same way you started the first thread, being sure to tie your new thread on over the other threads.

To change to a color that is already tied into the wrap, simply drop the color you're working with and pick up the new color.

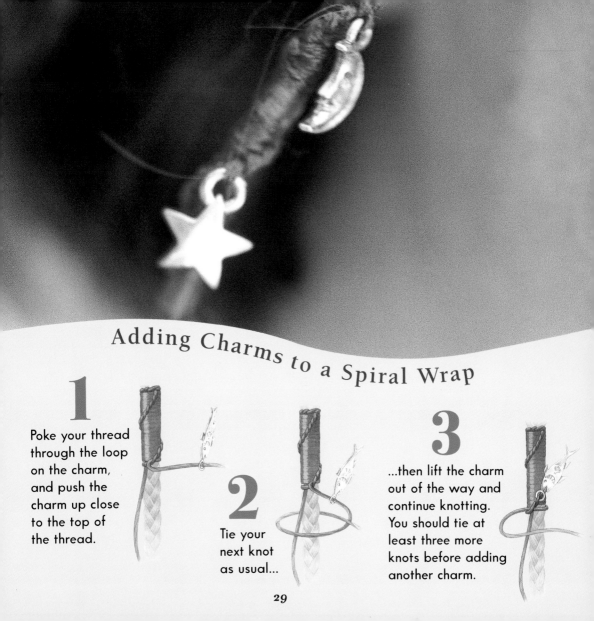

Adding Charms to a Spiral Wrap

1

Poke your thread through the loop on the charm, and push the charm up close to the top of the thread.

2

Tie your next knot as usual...

3

...then lift the charm out of the way and continue knotting. You should tie at least three more knots before adding another charm.

**Book Design and
Graphic Production:**
Kevin Plottner

Art Direction:
MaryEllen Podgorski

Illustrations:
Darwen &
Vally Hennings

Photography:
Thomas Heinser
Peter Fox

Write us

We want to hear your comments about this, or any Klutz book. We've even given you a postcard to make it easy. We **always** read **all** our mail.

You can also use this card to get a copy of **The Klutz Catalogue** — a complete listing of all the fine books we publish. Here's how you do it:

1 Cut out. **2** Fill in. **3** Add stamp. **4** Mail (important). **5** Wait impatiently. We'll take care of the rest.

Who Are You?

Name: _____

Address: _____

City: _____ State: _____ Zip: _____

Tell us more...

❑ I'm a kid. I was born in the year: _____

❑ According to my birth certificate, I'm a grownup. But I deny it.

How did you first hear about this book? _____

Tell us what you think:

```
┌─────────────────────────────────────────────┐
│                                               │
│                                               │
│                                               │
│                                               │
│                                               │
└─────────────────────────────────────────────┘
```

❑ Your complaints (please do not write outside the box).

What would **you** like us to write a book about?

_____

❑ Check this box if you want to have a look at The Klutz Catalogue.

More Great Books from **KLUTZ**

Beads: A Book of
Ideas & Instructions

Boondoggle: A Book
of Lanyard & Lacing

The Incredible Clay Book

Friendship Bracelets

Country & Blues Guitar
for the Musically Hopeless

Hair: A Book of
Braiding & Styles

Nail Art

Smoothies: 22 Frosty Fruit Drinks

String Games from
Around the World

Watercolor for the
Artistically Undiscovered

First Class
Postage
Here

KLUTZ®

455 Portage Avenue
Palo Alto, CA 94306